NEW YORK 2014

THE CITY AT A GLANCE

G000294386

Manhattan Municipal Building
Adolph Alexander Weinman's golde
Civic Fame tops McKim, Mead & W
1914 Beaux Arts government offic
It was the first building in New Yo
to incorporate a subway station.
1 Centre Street

Brooklyn Bridge
Fly into JFK Airport and no doubt this is how
you'll cross the East River to arrive downtown.
It was designed by John Augustus Roebling,
who died before its completion in 1883.

Empire State Building
Architect William Lamb's skyscraper (King
Kong's favourite New York high-rise) opened
to the public in 1931. The views from the
86th-floor observatory really are fabulous.
350 Fifth Avenue, T 212 736 3100

Chrysler Building
The ornamentation on William Van Alen's
1930 art deco gem was inspired by the
radiators and hubcaps of Chrysler cars.
405 Lexington Avenue

United Nations
This outstanding International Style complex,
with the Secretariat tower as its centrepiece, is
based on the designs of 11 architects. A massive
renovation project, which will run up a bill of
about $2bn, is scheduled to finish in 2015.
405 E 42nd Street

Manhattan Bridge
Connecting Manhattan and Brooklyn, Ralph
Modjeski and Leon Moisseiff's bridge, opened
in 1909, now carries seven lanes of traffic and
four subway tracks. An $834m reconstruction,
focused on improving safety and reducing
congestion, is due for completion by 2014.

INTRODUCTION
THE CHANGING FACE OF THE URBAN SCENE

Is New York the greatest city on earth? Probably, although London would like to vie for that mantle too. There's certainly a buoyant atmosphere in the Big Apple right now. Real estate is selling, the dining scene is running at full throttle, and the creative industries are celebrating homegrown talent and, in some cases, supporting local manufacturing (see p084). The stealth wealth of a decade or so ago has been tempered, though, and Gothamites are showing an appreciation for originality and provenance. Retailers selling hand-crafted or artisanal goods, and restaurants presenting farm-to-table, even roof-to-table (see p050) menus tap into the demand for products with an innate sense of place. The glamour and the glitz are still discernible, of course, only now New Yorkers expect something more authentic for their buck.

Since the tragedy of 9/11, New York has slowly but steadily rediscovered its enthusiasm for the new. Manhattan's West Side is currently the location of an ambitious regeneration scheme, the Hudson Yards Project (see p064), while the reimagined World Trade Center site (see p010) is reconfiguring the downtown skyline, structure by structure. Elsewhere, artists and hipsters continue to migrate to the less well-trodden districts of Brooklyn (the likes of Williamsburg and Park Slope are now as expensive and elitist as Tribeca or Nolita) and, increasingly, to Queens. Formerly on the fringes, these boroughs are becoming the epicentres of cool.

ESSENTIAL INFO
FACTS, FIGURES AND USEFUL ADDRESSES

TOURIST OFFICE
810 Seventh Avenue
T 212 484 1222
www.nycgo.com

TRANSPORT
Airport transfer to Manhattan
AirTrains run 24 hours to the subway and
Long Island Rail Road, which links to Penn
Station. The journey takes 50 minutes
www.panynj.gov/airports/jfk-airtrain.html
Car hire
Avis
T 212 593 8396
Car service
Dial 7 Car & Limousine Service
T 212 777 7777
MetroCard
A seven-day Metro and bus pass costs $55
www.mta.info/metrocard
Subway
Trains run 24 hours a day, every day
www.mta.info
Yellow cabs
T 212 639 9675
(for enquiries such as lost property)

EMERGENCY SERVICES
Emergencies
T 911
Police (non-emergency)
T 311
24-hour pharmacy
CVS
630 Lexington Avenue
T 917 369 8688

CONSULATES
British Consulate-General
845 Third Avenue
T 212 745 0200
www.gov.uk/government/world/usa

POSTAL SERVICES
Post office
90 Church Street
T 1 800 275 8777
Shipping
UPS
T 212 680 3118

BOOKS
**Block by Block: Jane Jacobs and
the Future of New York**
(Princeton Architectural Press)
Here is New York by EB White
(Little Bookroom)
Long Island Modernism 1930–1980
by Caroline Rob Zaleski (WW Norton & Co)

WEBSITES
Architecture/Design
www.cooperhewitt.org
Newspaper
www.nytimes.com

EVENTS
Frieze Art Fair
www.friezenewyork.com
ICFF
www.icff.com
NYCxDESIGN
nycxdesign.com

COST OF LIVING
Taxi from JFK Airport to Manhattan
$60
Cappuccino
$3.50
Packet of cigarettes
$12
Daily newspaper
$2.50
Bottle of champagne
$65

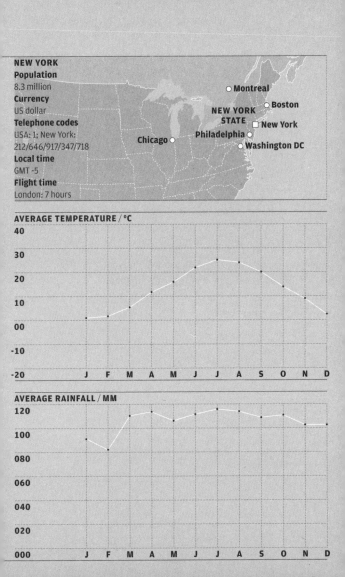

NEW YORK
Population
8.3 million
Currency
US dollar
Telephone codes
USA: 1; New York:
212/646/917/347/718
Local time
GMT -5
Flight time
London: 7 hours

Montreal
Boston
NEW YORK
STATE ☐ New York
Chicago
Philadelphia
Washington DC

AVERAGE TEMPERATURE / °C

40

30

20

10

00

-10

-20
    J   F   M   A   M   J   J   A   S   O   N   D

AVERAGE RAINFALL / MM

120

100

080

060

040

020

000
    J   F   M   A   M   J   J   A   S   O   N   D

NEIGHBOURHOODS

THE AREAS YOU NEED TO KNOW AND WHY

To help you navigate the city, we've chosen the most interesting districts (see below and the map inside the back cover) and colour-coded our featured venues, according to their location; those venues that are outside these areas are not coloured.

TRIBECA/THE BATTERY

Manhattan's southern end could not be more diverse. Downtown's most compelling area, Ground Zero (see p010), is still under construction more than a decade after 9/11. Tribeca is a younger version of Soho, with sophisticated restaurants such as Atera (see p052) and Brushstroke (see p053).

UPPER WEST SIDE

Archetypal liberal intellectual territory, this residential district benefits from old and new money. The vast Central Park West apartment blocks are like ocean liners steaming through Manhattan. Its cultural focal point is Lincoln Center (see p066), which was recently renovated.

WEST VILLAGE

Darling of both indie and global brands (especially along Bleecker Street), the leafy West Village has a vibrant yet intimate ambience. Here, Manhattan assumes a human scale, with cosy neighbourhood eateries, 19th-century townhouses and pretty streets, such as Perry and Charles.

SOHO

Once an artists' quarter, where cast-iron buildings were transformed into post-industrial lofts and studios, the vibe is now more Kenzo than De Kooning, and Soho can feel like a tourist trap. However, it does have cool stores, such as Kiosk (see p077), good galleries and boutique hotels, including The James (see p029).

UPPER EAST SIDE

This is quintessential rich-bitch New York, replete with liveried doormen helping social X-rays carry bag upon bag after a hard day's shopping on Madison. It's also where you'll find the city's most important museums. Newcomers include Arlington Club (see p038) and Hospoda (see p049).

MIDTOWN

Manhattan's central business district is the home of Times Square – the backdrop for the bright lights of Broadway or a tacky, neon-lit, tourist hell, depending on your take. Architectural highlights include the Museum of Arts and Design (2 Columbus Circle, T 212 299 7777).

CHELSEA

The unmissable attraction here is the High Line (see p036); Chelsea is also an epicentre for heavyweight art galleries. Modish venues like Hôtel Americano (see p017) and its rooftop bar, La Piscine (see p054), have helped to restore a hipness that gentrification had diminished.

EAST VILLAGE/LOWER EAST SIDE

Traditionally a working-class, immigrant area, the Lower East Side is still a cultural melting pot, and home to some of NYC's edgier art spaces and bars, as well as SANAA's New Museum (see p065). To the north, the East Village has been heading upmarket since the 1980s, while Noho draws fashionistas to its trendy boutiques.

LANDMARKS

THE SHAPE OF THE CITY SKYLINE

How can you pick out a landmark building in a city that possibly contains more instantly recognisable skyscrapers than any other? Perhaps owing to its relative youth, New York has never been shy about making a statement with modern architecture. And thanks to the wealth of many of its citizens, the Big Apple has been able to call on the talents of almost every architect of note over the past 100 or so years, to create its incomparable skyline.

Amid the cranes, congestion and altercations of Ground Zero, the new World Trade Center site, a modified version of Daniel Libeskind's original master plan, is an ongoing project. At its heart lies Michael Arad and Peter Walker and Partners' plaza (overleaf), featuring two huge waterfalls positioned in the footprints of the Twin Towers. Between them, opening in 2014, will be Davis Brody Bond's subterranean National September 11 Memorial Museum (Albany Street/Greenwich Street, T 212 266 5211), entered via Snøhetta's glass pavilion. Rearing above this, two of the site's five main towers have topped out: the 514m 1 WTC (West Street/Vesey Street), by SOM's David Childs, which is vying for the title of tallest building in the western hemisphere; and the more quietly impressive 298m 4 WTC (150 Greenwich Street), by Fumihiko Maki. Santiago Calatrava's transportation hub is underway, and there are plans for a performing arts centre, designed by Frank Gehry. *For full addresses, see Resources.*

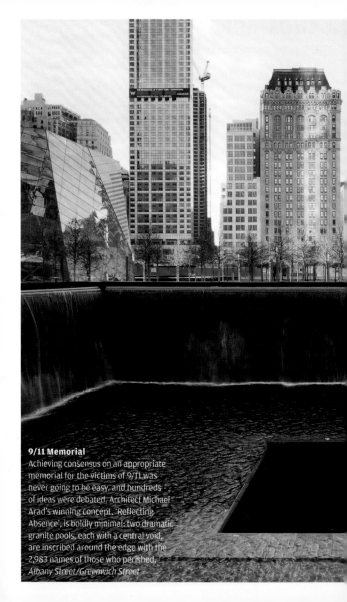

9/11 Memorial

Achieving consensus on an appropriate memorial for the victims of 9/11 was never going to be easy, and hundreds of ideas were debated. Architect Michael Arad's winning concept, 'Reflecting Absence', is boldly minimal: two dramatic granite pools, each with a central void, are inscribed around the edge with the 2,983 names of those who perished. *Albany Street/Greenwich Street*

AT&T Building

This massive 1932 art deco structure, designed by American architect Ralph Walker, was originally known as the AT&T Long Distance Building; it housed the telecommunications giant's transatlantic offices and equipment. In the 1990s, the company made this its HQ, although AT&T has since sold up. Its brick-clad bulk (all 106,838 sq m of it) is quintessentially Gotham-like in form, and the lobby boasts the obligatory tiled map of the world on one wall. The building may not be one of the city's best-known landmarks, nor even Walker's best work (this is usually said to be the former Irving Trust Company headquarters at 1 Wall Street). However, from its profile to the materials used, the AT&T could not be found anywhere except New York, and for that it is a masterwork. *32 Sixth Avenue, www.32sixthave.com*

Hearst Tower

Fresh from remodelling London's skyline with 30 St Mary Axe (the Gherkin), Norman Foster tackled the HQ of the Hearst media empire. The diamond-faceted facade of this 46-storey tower, completed in 2006, thrusts out of an existing art deco building that was commissioned in the 1920s by media mogul William Randolph Hearst; the six-storey structure was always intended to form the base of a landmark high-rise.

The new blends seamlessly with the old, thanks to the dramatic lobby that extends up through the lower floors to provide access to all parts of the building. And it's not just a pretty sight. The tower is environmentally friendly too – it was constructed with more than 85 per cent recycled steel and consumes about a quarter less energy than its neighbours. *300 W 57th Street, www.hearst.com*

Austrian Cultural Forum

In a city where bigger is often thought to be better, Austrian architect Raimund Abraham created a diminutive wonder in 2002 with his first major US project, although he had lived in New York for more than 30 years. 'My intention was to resolve the extreme condition of the smallness of the site,' he said. The architect, who died in 2010, succeeded. The Cultural Forum is a brilliant design: a glass-skinned sliver, a mere 7.6m wide, rising to 85m. Its presence belies its dimensions, and the ACFNY's brooding facade – reminiscent, in profile, of an Easter Island statue – outshines all the surrounding buildings. When it was unveiled, it was hailed by many as the most important structure to have been erected in Manhattan in four decades. *11 E 52nd Street, T 212 319 5300, www.acfny.org*

Woolworth Building

For some 17 years after its opening in 1913, Cass Gilbert's Woolworth Building was the tallest in the world. His client, five-and-dime-store magnate Frank W Woolworth, was wealthy enough to pay the $13.5m price tag in cash. This, coupled with the structure's gothic proportions, earned it the moniker 'the cathedral of commerce'. Even today, the sheer scale of the building is awe-inspiring: it stands at 241.4m high, and there's room for 14,000 office workers across 54 floors, all of which are served by 30 elevators. The top 30 floors are currently being converted into a handful of apartments. In the spectacular lobby, which is lined with marble and lavishly decorated with mosaics and bronze, there are medieval-style gargoyles, including caricatures of Woolworth and Gilbert.
233 Broadway

HOTELS

WHERE TO STAY AND WHICH ROOMS TO BOOK

The luxury boutique hotel is back with a bang in NYC. Openings across town include the Refinery Hotel (63 W 38th Street, T 646 664 0310), a 1920s-themed property that took over a hat factory in the Garment District, and The Quin (101 W 57th Street, T 212 600 2108), which launched in the former 1929 Buckingham Hotel, south of Central Park. Heading downtown, we admire The Jade (see p018), a quiet hideaway in Greenwich Village.

Although Midtown is an unquestionably convenient location, the sheer number of hotels here is overwhelming. If cost is not a consideration, check into the Four Seasons (see p023), where the finely tuned service rarely misses a step. On the Upper East Side, The Surrey (20 E 76th Street, T 212 288 3700) is a good base for Frieze Art Fair, and has the added advantages of a top-flight restaurant, Café Boulud (T 212 772 2600), and spa (see p089).

The creative set still flocks to Williamsburg's Wythe Hotel (see p026), a hop and a skip from a string of hip restaurants and bars. On Manhattan's Lower East Side, The Nolitan (see p028) and the Thompson LES (190 Allen Street, T 212 460 5300) are both strong options. The latter's upscale take on Japanese pub food at Blue Ribbon Sushi Izakaya (T 212 466 0404) is a real draw. If you're in the city on business, book a room at the Andaz Wall Street (see p022), arguably the slickest reservation in the financial district. *For full addresses and room rates, see Resources.*

Hôtel Americano
Tucked within Chelsea's gallery district, Grupo Habita's first American hotel is a class act, from architect Enrique Norten's mesh-covered building to the sleek interiors created by Parisian designer Arnaud Montigny. The 56 rooms exude urban cool, with low platform beds and contemporary furnishings in a palette of black, grey and yellow; the ninth-floor Studio Suite (above) is among the best.

The rooftop lounge, La Piscine (see p054), serves up crisp cocktails and knockout views of the High Line (see p036), while downstairs, in The Americano restaurant (T 212 525 0000), chef Joseph Buenconsejo creates zippy French cuisine with Latin touches. The vibe is laidback but full of brio, especially during Sunday brunch. *518 W 27th Street, T 212 216 0000, www.hotel-americano.com*

The Jade Hotel

Launched in 2013, The Jade was hotly anticipated due to the lack of attractive hotels in this neighbourhood. Colombia-born Andres Escobar took his cue for the interiors from 1920s Paris, decorating the 113 rooms (Standard, above), and public areas, like the lobby (opposite), with rich tones and furnishings inspired by that era's most glamorous designer, Émile-Jacques Ruhlmann. There are only five to seven rooms on each of the 18 floors, reinforcing the intimate feel. The art deco theme is carried over to the bar/restaurant, Grape & Vine, which is run by French football star Youri Djorkaeff and the restaurateur Frederick Lesort. The cocktails are spirited and strong, and the new American menu is underpinned by artisanal ingredients.
52 W 13th Street, T 212 375 1300, www.thejadenyc.com

Ace Hotel

In 2009, the first East Coast offshoot of this Seattle-based chain signalled the start of more design-savvy times for the Nomad area. Playing on the Americana theme, with vintage and custom-made furnishings, NYC's Roman and Williams created a look that still feels cool. Check into Loft 811 (pictured) and brush up in Rudy's Barbershop (see p094).
20 W 29th Street, T 212 679 2222

Andaz Wall Street

Wall Street seems like a logical location for a full-service, luxury hotel, but previous efforts have either fallen short or failed outright. The Andaz, designed by David Rockwell, is Hyatt's attempt, making the most of a prime position and learning from its predecessors' missteps. Housed in a former Barclays Bank building, dating to 1982, the hotel's standard lobby and check-in desk have been replaced by a lounge with an iPad-wielding host. The 253 rooms are large and well proportioned. We opted for Room 1513 (above), looking on to Wall Street; those facing south-west overlook Hanover Square. The cuisine in Wall & Water (T 212 699 1700), the Andaz's mod-American restaurant, is tasty, so you will be grateful for the lower-level gym.
75 Wall Street, T 212 590 1234,
www.andaz.com

Four Seasons

It's the Four Seasons, so of course it's impeccable. Perhaps the Canadian group's crown jewel, the IM Pei-designed tower is still said to be the city's tallest hotel, and by golly does the Chinese-born architect give good power lobby. The service is exemplary, and as for the rooms, they may not all be to our taste but they are large and luxurious; the 400 sq m Ty Warner Penthouse (above), is stunning (and pricey, being one of the world's most expensive hotel suites). At a pinch, we think the views looking north over Central Park are the best, but the southern aspect is pretty impressive too. Cap off your day in an oversized chair by the fireplace in the Ty Lounge with a perfect martini and some gripping people-watching.
57 E 57th Street, T 212 758 5700,
www.fourseasons.com/newyork

Crosby Street Hotel

Although it's right in the heart of the city, Crosby Street is one of those New York thoroughfares that feels off the radar. Rising 11 storeys above a former parking lot, the red-brick Crosby Street Hotel (the only American outpost for Britain's Firmdale Hotels group) feels old New York outside, new New York inside. In the lobby, which has full-height windows, Kit Kemp introduced colourful paintings and fabrics, and a monumental metal skull sculpture by Jaume Plensa. Vintage dressmaker's mannequins and oversized headboards set a quirky tone in the 86 rooms, which overlook Soho; opt for a One Bedroom Suite (above). Belly up to The Crosby Bar, decorated in a cheery style, for well-crafted cocktails and small plates. *79 Crosby Street, T 212 226 6400, www.firmdalehotels.com*

The NoMad Hotel

Injecting a shot of lavishness into Midtown, The NoMad marries old-world charm with New York sophistication in a turn-of-the-century Beaux Arts building. Attention to historical detail characterises Jacques Garcia's treatment of the 168 rooms and public areas, such as the lobby (above). Vintage Heriz rugs cover a salvaged maple floor, and the library's 200-year-old spiral staircase was imported from France.

Reserve one of the lofty Grande Rooms, or a Suite for a diverting street vista. The restaurant, NoMad (T 347 472 5660), is helmed by Will Guidara and Daniel Humm of Michelin-starred Eleven Madison Park (T 212 889 0905). Maison Kitsuné opened its first boutique in America on the ground floor (T 212 481 6010).

1170 Broadway, T 212 796 1500,
www.thenomadhotel.com

Wythe Hotel
Opened in 2012, the Wythe has given Brooklyn the grown-up hotel it deserves. The factory building has been wisely preserved, and the decor of reclaimed pine furniture and bespoke wallpaper (King Room, pictured) is the right foil, softening the industrial edge. Dine at Reynard (T 718 460 8004), then drink in the Manhattan skyline from the bar.
80 Wythe Avenue, T 718 460 8000

The Nolitan

Design firm Grzywinski+Pons were faced with the challenge of creating a sense of community within a community for the Nolita area's first boutique hotel. The result is an industrial-chic low-rise that blends in well with its surroundings. There are 55 snug rooms, with oak flooring, concrete ceilings, Corian accents and floor-to-ceiling windows; some have private balconies. The public spaces are generous: there's a sizeable roof terrace, and on the ground level, the lobby (above) connects to a library and a café. The many amenities (such as bikes and skateboards) are varied enough to attract both business travellers and trendsetters, and despite residing on a traffic-heavy street corner, the hotel maintains a tranquil atmosphere.
30 Kenmare Street, T 212 925 2555, www.nolitanhotel.com

The James

Designed by ODA in collaboration with Perkins Eastman, The James has a boxy, almost brutalist facade, and appears to float on stilts cantilevered above elegant terraced gardens. Inside, the aesthetic is just as daring, courtesy of in-house curator Matthew Jensen. Working with Artists Space, he has devoted each of the 14 floors to artists such as Aaron Wexler and Sun K Kwak. As for the rooms, dark wooden headboards rise above white beds, and there are rainshowers behind translucent screens. Accommodations are on the small side, although the massive windows let in plenty of light. Unwind by the rooftop pool (above), dropping down to the subterranean David Burke Kitchen (T 212 201 9119) for a bite to eat. *27 Grand Street, T 212 465 2000, www.jameshotel.com*

The Standard High Line

Like his classic Soho hotel, The Mercer
(T 212 966 6060), André Balazs' Standard
took a long time to see the light of day.
The 338-room tower finally opened in
2009, and, several years on, it has become
something of a landmark. Looming 18m
over the High Line (see p036), the hulking
slab of glass, perched on concrete pylons,
juts into the West Side skyline. Beyond
the lobby (above), the rooms are compact,
but benefit from this area's low-slung
warehouses, giving unobstructed city
or Hudson River views. Designers Roman
and Williams added elements such as
wood tambour panelling, which extends
up the rooms' walls and across the ceiling.
The Standard Grill (T 212 645 4100) and
Living Room bar still pull in a lively crowd.
848 Washington Street, T 212 645 4646,
www.standardhotels.com/high-line

The Chatwal

This 1905 building was originally designed by architect Stanford White. In 2010, it was overhauled by Thierry Despont, who applied his own updated version of art deco in dazzling fashion. The 76 guest rooms, including the grand Producer Suite (above), are decorated with vintage 'steamer trunk' wardrobes, fine suede walls and old subway signs. Off the lobby, in The Lambs Club restaurant (T 212 997 5262), Geoffrey Zakarian collects rave reviews for his modern American cuisine. The 18th-century French stone fireplace, red-leather banquettes and warm lighting make a handsome backdrop for the equally alluring food, which pairs like a charm with the cocktails created by NYC nightlife veteran Sasha Petraske.
130 W 44th Street, T 212 764 6200, www.thechatwalny.com

24 HOURS
SEE THE BEST OF THE CITY IN JUST ONE DAY

New York offers some of the best dining, sightseeing and shopping in the world. Head in any direction and you'll discover something intriguing within the first few blocks. So the problem is not how to fill a day, but what to fit in. Our suggested strategy is to focus on the must-sees, one trip at a time, since you'll obviously be back. For example, MoMA in Midtown (11 W 53rd Street, T 212 708 9400), Museum Mile on the east side of Central Park – including the Whitney (945 Madison Avenue, T 212 570 3600), the Met (1000 Fifth Avenue, T 212 535 7710) and the Guggenheim (1071 Fifth Avenue, T 212 423 3500) – and the glossy galleries of Chelsea are a few weekends' worth of culture alone. Then there are the shops (see p037 and p072): to come to NYC and not drop a coin would be like going to Amsterdam and not crossing a canal.

Rather than an attempt at the impossible, the day suggested here is a snapshot of New York through the eyes of a local. We recommend hopping between three of the city's five boroughs, all connected by short subway rides, to get a taste of how rich and diverse these areas are. Start with breakfast in Brooklyn and then continue with an afternoon split between Queens and Manhattan. Wrap up with a spirited steakhouse dinner on the Upper East Side and sultry late-night cocktails downtown. Not everything will be to everyone's taste, but how will you know until you've tried? *For full addresses, see Resources.*

10.00 Runner & Stone

Bread is having a moment in New York, thanks, in part, to a group of artisan bakers elevating the humble loaf. At Runner & Stone in Gowanus, owners Chris Pizzulli, who hailed from Blue Ribbon (see p062), and Peter Endriss, formerly of Bouchon Bakery (T 212 823 9366) and Per Se (T 212 823 9335), focus on all things baked. For breakfast, order the baguette, plain or buckwheat, served with freshly churned butter – great on its own, but even more delicious with a mug of Crop to Cup coffee. Manhattan architects Latent Productions repurposed some 1,000 empty flour sacks to line the walls in a brick-like formation, and design group Withers & Grain salvaged wood from old Brooklyn water towers to construct the tables and chairs.
285 3rd Avenue, T 718 576 3360, www.runnerandstone.com

12.00 MoMA PS1

Consider PS1 to be the cooler cousin of the main MoMA (see p032). Housed in an 1893 neo-Romanesque schoolhouse, renovated by LA architects Frederick Fisher, this more adventurous arm of the museum dedicates itself solely to contemporary art. There's a palpable energy throughout the venue, created in part by the architecture – the old building is juxtaposed with site-specific installations, inside and out. The Long Island City location, an area garnering more and more attention, adds to the appeal. PS1's activities range from programmes for young architects and artists to live events. Culinary trendsetters Hugue Dufour and Sarah Obraitis head up M Wells Dinette, a great place for lunch. Closed Tuesdays and Wednesdays. *22-25 Jackson Avenue, T 718 784 2084, www.momaps1.org*

14.00 High Line

A green strip of elevated parkway in West Manhattan has been the regeneration project on everyone's lips for the past few years. This abandoned 1930s rail track was threatened with demolition in the late 1990s, prompting two local residents, Robert Hammond and Joshua David, to form a non-profit group, Friends of the High Line, to save it. The result, designed by architects Diller Scofidio + Renfro, and

James Corner Field Operations, is an inspired public space, used from dawn till dusk. The first section, from Gansevoort Street to W 20th Street, opened in 2009, and a second section, extending to W 30th Street, was finished in 2011. Its final phase, the High Line at the Rail Yards, is due to open in 2014 and will run to W 34th Street, wrapping around Hudson Yards (see p064). *T 212 500 6035, www.thehighline.org*

16.00 Proenza Schouler

In 2012, designers Lazaro Hernandez and Jack McCollough took their downtown style, adored by art and fashion folk, uptown, with their first flagship store. To carve out a suitably edgy boutique amid Madison Avenue's tony storefronts, the duo enlisted their friend, British architect David Adjaye, who also designed their showroom. The townhouse space, split over two levels – a mix of glass, wood, concrete and steel – has a minimal aesthetic that lets the clothes, accessories and other exclusive creations shine. If you're in the mood to invest, plump for one of the many versions of the PS1 bag. Launched in 2008, it's an elegant take on the messenger style, and is now a contemporary classic. Closed Sundays. *822 Madison Avenue, T 212 585 3200, www.proenzaschouler.com*

20.00 Arlington Club

Steakhouses are a New York institution, but all too many of them are stodgy and dated. Enter Arlington Club, a zippy newcomer on the Upper East Side launched by French chef Laurent Tourondel, in partnership with the Tao Group. Its menu combines impeccable meaty offerings (all steaks are dry-aged for 28 days) with Japanese elements, such as pristine plates of sushi. Designed by ICRAVE, the Beaux Arts inspired dining room, featuring gold flourishes, dark furnishings, chandeliers and an arched glass-and-steel ceiling that evokes the original Penn Station, has a great atmosphere, exuding the kind of buzz that will entice you back. Request a table on the second level for the best view of everything and everyone. The restaurant has been packed since its launch in late 2012, so reserve a table well in advance.
1032 Lexington Avenue, T 212 249 5700, www.arlingtonclubny.com

URBAN LIFE
CAFÉS, RESTAURANTS, BARS AND NIGHTCLUBS

The newest restaurants and bars reflect an optimistic, resourceful mood. Small plates still dominate, and the elaborate tasting menu at Atera (see p052) tops our list. For a more moderate bill, try Pearl & Ash (see p042), the Asian-style comfort food at Tribeca Canvas (313 Church Street, T 917 720 2845), or updated Italian classics at the hip Carbone (181 Thompson Street, T 212 254 3000).

Brooklyn, and lately Queens, are booming, giving Manhattanites plenty of reasons to venture off the island. Chef and Queens native Joel Reiss delivers big, bold steaks at S Prime (35-15 36th Street, T 718 707 0660) in Long Island City; and Fredrik Berselius takes diners on a Scandinavian sortie at Aska in Williamsburg (90 Wythe Avenue, T 718 388 2969). Greenpoint is also garnering attention, and now boasts River Styx (21 Greenpoint Avenue), the second restaurant from the team behind Roebling Tea Room (143 Roebling Street, T 718 963 0760), and Luksus (615 Manhattan Avenue, T 718 389 6034), in the back room of Tørst, the area's cool craft-beer bar.

There's no shortage of spirited bars in New York, and those with glittering views lure locals and tourists alike. Sip cocktails at the sophisticated Center Bar (Fourth floor, 10 Columbus Circle, T 212 823 9482), overlooking Central Park, or for a louder, livelier scene, hop on the L Train to The Ides at the Wythe Hotel (see p026), from where you can contemplate Manhattan.

For full addresses, see Resources.

Antica Pesa

The first outpost of the renowned Roman restaurant, opened in 1922, serves *cucina rustica* in a refined setting, bringing a refreshing urbanity to Williamsburg and its dining scene. The interior designers, Brooklyn-based BArC Studio, created three distinct zones: the front area caters to larger groups; the middle section has a marble bar and snug lounge with a fireplace; and to the rear is the main dining room, featuring walnut wood, white walls and pendant lights. Order one or two of the pastas, which are superb. *Schiaffoni all'amatriciana* (with cured pork jowl, crushed tomatoes and pecorino) and spaghetti *cacio e pepe* (with parmesan, pecorino and black pepper) are brilliantly executed versions of the Roman classics. *115 Berry Street, T 347 763 2635, www.anticapesa.com*

Pearl & Ash
Chef Richard Kuo heads up the tiny
kitchen at Pearl & Ash, serving small
plates with big flavours from around
the world. The interiors, by Brooklyn's
Sway Design Collective, comprise poplar
tables along a wall lined with a display
of moss and ephemera. Linger at the
bar with a glass from the extensive wine
list or one of Eben Klemm's cocktails.
220 Bowery, T 212 837 2370

Talde

Food trends come and go, but Dale Talde is on a mission to bring one, pan-Asian, back into favour. And the long queues and good reviews at his Park Slope restaurant prove that Talde (formerly of Manhattan's Morimoto and Buddakan) is succeeding. The characterful canteen has mahogany carvings from a Pennsylvanian antiques warehouse, and window frames and mantelpieces salvaged in New York from an early 20th-century mansion's oriental study. The intricately carved dragons and samurai warriors are by Maeda Yasube Yoshitsugu, known for his work on Japanese shrines in the mid-19th century. The menu is a tasty Asian tour via dishes such as pretzel pork and chive dumplings, and crispy oyster and bacon pad thai.
369 7th Avenue, T 347 916 0031, www.taldebrooklyn.com

Potlikker

Redesigned comfort food is the speciality at chef Liza Queen's popular restaurant on Williamsburg's south side. Rather than following a singular culinary tradition, Queen, who headed over to Vietnam for ideas after closing her first venture, The Queen's Hideaway, concentrates on unexpected flavour combinations. One highly addictive dish is her Dutch pancake, which is airy and light, and smothered in goat's cheese, homemade hot-pepper jelly, crispy bacon and fried oysters. Queen's sister, designer Samantha Crasco (who decorated the Greenwich Hotel's guest rooms), broke away from the ubiquitous ramshackle Brooklyn aesthetic, lending Potlikker a clean-lined and cheerful look. The curved wooden bar is particularly cool. *338 Bedford Avenue, T 718 388 9808, www.potlikkerbrooklyn.com*

Alder
One of the hottest tables in town since
its launch in March 2013, Alder is helmed
by molecular gastronomy pioneer Wylie
Dufresne, who has created a menu
of whimsically deconstructed classics.
Jennifer Carpenter's interior features
a textured brick wall, and a ceiling made
from salvaged fencing, which is hung
at varying angles for a wave-like effect.
157 Second Avenue, T 212 539 1900

Momofuku Ssäm Bar

Korean-American David Chang seemingly came out of nowhere to establish himself as one of New York's most exciting chefs. His cluster of restaurants includes the Midtown Má Pêche (T 212 757 5878) and a trio of East Village venues, among them the flagship Momofuku Ssäm Bar. Injecting new vigour into the played-out pan-Asian genre, Chang's food celebrates the colours, flavours and textures of the orient, and presents some unexpected flourishes. Long, narrow and sleek, with stools and communal tables, MSB does not take reservations, but any queueing is worth the wait, we assure you. Try the signature steamed pork buns, which are stuffed with crisp pork strips, hoisin sauce, spring onions and gherkins.
207 Second Avenue, T 212 254 3500, www.momofuku.com

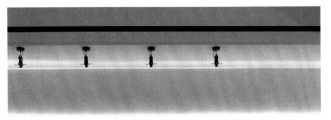

Hospoda

A *hospoda* is a traditional Czech beer hall, but this Upper East Side restaurant is far from commonplace. Designer Vaclav Cervenka of the Prague-based Ateliér ph5 conceived a striking decor, where the work of Czech graffiti artist Jakub Matuska (aka Masker) covers the walls, and there's a dramatic glass and stainless-steel bar. A rarity in the world of fine dining, Hospoda has proved a hit with both beer and food lovers. A cutting-edge tap called the Quadrunner allows you to enjoy one of the best-known Czech lagers, Pilsner Urquell, in four different ways, depending on how the glass is tilted and the amount of foam that is created. Chefs Katie Busch and Oldrich Sahajdak have devised an inspired menu of Czech-inflected dishes. *321 E 73rd Street, T 212 861 1038, www.hospodanyc.com*

Rosemary's

Farm-to-table food is all too familiar now, but how about roof-to-table? At this Greenwich Avenue trattoria, launched by Carlos Suarez, owner of the nearby Bobo (T 212 488 2626), ingredients are plucked from the rooftop garden and cooked within minutes – as evidenced in the minestrone, a broth brimming with fresh herbs, tomatoes and baby vegetables. Chef Wade Moises, formerly of Babbo (T 212 777 0303), also turns out fantastic pastas and fluffy focaccia among other Italian delicacies. Dekar Design installed greenery, pale wooden furniture and lights strung from the ceiling beams to give the lofty space a casual, relaxed feel. The super-fresh food, relatively gentle pricing and airy urban-farmhouse decor have kept Rosemary's packed day and night since it opened in June 2012.

18 Greenwich Avenue, T 212 647 1818,
www.rosemarysnyc.com

Atera

It's all about the journey at Matthew Lightner's acclaimed, 18-seat temple to the tasting menu. First, finding Atera can be tricky, as it's located in an unmarked commercial building. Once you're here, the three-hour gastronomic adventure begins. Design firm Parts & Labor used reclaimed wood for the ceiling and slate in the kitchen, softened by a vertical garden on the back wall. The menu changes regularly, but Lightner's technical prowess and visual imagination are present in every morsel, from the starters (mini lobster rolls in a toasted yeast meringue) to the desserts (churros made of salsify). If you can't get a reservation in the restaurant, try The Lounge below, which serves up cocktails and Lightner's bar snacks.
77 Worth Street, T 212 226 1444, www.ateranyc.com

Brushstroke

For his latest venture, housed in an 1860s brick building in Tribeca, famed New York chef/restaurateur David Bouley teamed up with Osaka's Tsuji Culinary Institute. The house speciality is *kaiseki*: a multi-course, seasonal, traditional Japanese meal that requires years of training to master. To keep the chefs' preparations as the focal point, Tokyo-based design firm Super Potato devised an airy, clean-lined dining room, choosing warm blondwood for the walls, floors, tables and chairs. An L-shaped bar cradles the open kitchen to maintain transparency between cooks and diners. The windows, on the other hand, are lined with rice paper to filter light and ensure privacy. Bouley added a sushi bar in 2012, helmed by Eiji Ichimura. *30 Hudson Street, T 212 791 3771, www.davidbouley.com*

La Piscine

Mix a dose of Mexican hospitality with a dash of French seduction, and you get this impossibly cool pool lounge crowning Hôtel Americano (see p017). Named after the 1969 film starring Romy Schneider and Alain Delon, La Piscine radiates nonchalant glamour. The main area is furnished, for the most part, with Brazilian furniture from Espasso (T 212 219 0017), and retractable glass walls mean the restaurant area can host diners all year. Joseph Buenconsejo's Greek-inspired summer menu is based on simple grilled seafood, meats and salads; winter dishes have an Alpine edge. The cocktail bar serves delicious libations and a long list of mescals. You don't have to enter the hotel to reach La Piscine – an exterior lift whisks you straight up.
Hôtel Americano, 518 W 27th Street, T 212 525 0000, www.hotel-americano.com

Miss Lily's

This energetic Caribbean joint, designed by New York nightlife impresario Serge Becker (Joe's Pub, La Esquina, The Box), is a whole lot of fun. The front dining room is tiny – just 20 tables and an abbreviated bar – but the city's stylish set congregate in the dimly lit, loungey back room. The decor, inspired by Brooklyn's traditional Jamaican chicken joints, is a mishmash of chequerboard floors, laminate booths and album-covered walls. There's a pulsing ska and reggae soundtrack, and the gorgeous staff sizzle as much as the dishes that they serve, like fiery jerk chicken, and cod fritters. Pop next door to record shop/café Miss Lily's Bake Shop, incorporating Melvin's Juice Box, which is helmed by New York juicing legend Melvin Major Jr. *132 W Houston Street, T 646 588 5375, www.misslilysnyc.com*

The Third Man

This Alphabet City cocktail den is a project by chefs Eduard Frauneder and Wolfgang Ban of the nearby Edi & The Wolf (T 212 598 1040) and Midtown's Michelin-starred Seäsonal (T 212 957 5550). A seductive mix of emerald-green booths, exposed brick, distressed mirrors, and spot lighting, The Third Man pays homage to Adolf Loos' legendary American Bar in Vienna, and Graham Greene's 1949 noir classic. The cocktails are evocative too, revealing the owners' passion for food and their attention to detail. The Franz Ferdinand is delectable: a shaken, brightly hued mix of fresh beetroot and blood-orange juices and Aperol, finished with an Austrian sparkling wine. If you're peckish, try some of the bar's fine charcuterie and cheese plates. *116 Avenue C, T 212 598 1040, www.thethirdmannyc.com*

Red Rooster

Whatever the time of day, there's always a buzz at Marcus Samuelsson's restaurant, which is situated in the heart of Harlem. The personality of the Ethiopian-born, Swedish-raised chef is reflected in the upbeat interior, lined with art by Sanford Biggers, Ming Smith and Philip Maysles. Usually packed to the gills, the venue attracts a diverse crowd, whether it's to the dining room (opposite), grocery (above) or the bar. The global menu is unique; try some crispy yardbird (fried chicken), Helga's meatballs, or dirty rice and shrimp. Sunday brunch is a raucous, no-reservations affair, when a gospel singer weaves amid diners. Downstairs, Ginny's Supper Club (T 212 421 3821) offers a blend of live music, cocktails and food. *310 Lenox Avenue, T 212 792 9001, www.redroosterharlem.com*

Donna

Despite its location in a quieter corner of south Williamsburg, Donna has become a destination for cocktail and design devotees. Aiming for a laidback, Central American atmosphere, the owner, Leif Huckman, partnered with the Haslegrave brothers from Brooklyn-based design firm hOmE to create a distinctive interior in this mid-19th-century building. The white walls and vaulted ceiling, salvaged pine flooring from Tall Cotton Supply, delicate steel light fixtures (a Haslegrave speciality), and hand-tiled bar stools all channel a Spanish colonial mood. Bar manager Jeremy Oertel's cocktails pay homage to Huckman's Honduran roots. Pair the tequila-based Fiery Dame or menthol amaro-infused Brancolada with tacos from the Brooklyn Taco Company, which is on-site Thursdays to Saturdays.
27 Broadway, T 646 568 6622, www.donnabklyn.com

INSIDER'S GUIDE

ANDREA MARY MARSHALL, ARTIST

After graduating from Parsons and a job in fashion, Boston-born Andrea Mary Marshall decamped to Bushwick, Brooklyn, where she discovered her calling as a self-portrait artist. While her work is provocative, she finds equilibrium in her neighbourhood: 'I like the solitude of where I live and work, and the quiet on my street.'

A pescatarian, Marshall is a longtime fan of Manhattan's Bread (20 Spring Street, T 212 334 1015) and its Sicilian tuna and fennel salad – 'I've been going there since I was 18.' She also singles out the macrobiotic Jappa soup at Souen (326 E 6th Street, T 212 388 1155), and sushi at Blue Ribbon (97 Sullivan Street, T 212 274 0404). Her love of spices is satiated with the classic Mexican food at El Parador Café (325 E 34th Street, T 212 679 6812) and in Manhattan's Koreatown. To unwind over drinks, she keeps it low-key: 'Milano's (51 E Houston Street, T 212 226 8844) in Nolita is a great dive bar.'

Given her intense feelings about art, Marshall likes to gallery hop on her own. She routinely tours the Met and MoMA (see p032), as well as edgier independents such as Salon 94 Bowery (243 Bowery, T 212 979 0001), Gavin Brown's Enterprise (620 Greenwich Street, T 212 627 5258) and Lehmann Maupin (540 W 26th Street, T 212 255 2923). If she isn't working at the weekend, Marshall takes a day trip to Brooklyn's Bay Ridge or Forest Hills in Queens, where 'you're in a completely different world'.

For full addresses, see Resources.

ARCHITOUR
A GUIDE TO NEW YORK'S ICONIC BUILDINGS

Chicago may be the birthplace of the skyscraper, Dubai may boast the world's tallest structure, and Shanghai may have more towers, but perhaps no city is as closely identified with the high-rise as New York. Money was the motivation to reach for the sky, but symbolism has always been immensely important here, from the automotive fantasies of the art deco Chrysler Building (405 Lexington Avenue) to the soaring silhouette of 1 WTC (see p009). Indeed, it may be Gothamites' inordinate love of towers that has enabled the city centre to retain its vibrancy, whereas so many of its American sister conurbations have become prisoners of suburban sprawl.

Right now, eyes are on the West Side, above 28th Street, where the redevelopment of this once gritty riverside zone is progressing. Kohn Pedersen Fox is master planner of the Hudson Yards Project (www.hydc.org), which will encompass mixed-use complexes, a subway extension and green space. Meanwhile, the debate rages about the future of New York Public Library, housed in Carrère and Hastings' landmark Beaux Arts building (42nd Street/Fifth Avenue, T 917 275 6975). Everyone agrees that something must be done to turn round its fortunes, the question is what. Norman Foster has published a modernisation plan, which is to install a lending library in the vault under the Rose Main Reading Room, but preservationists and some critics are unconvinced by his design. *For full addresses, see Resources.*

New Museum

It isn't often that an art space has much in common with a trash can. In actual fact, SANAA's New Museum of Contemporary Art, launched in 2007, may be the only building to be clad in the same wire mesh as its home city's trash receptacles. When the design – a series of piled-up silvery boxes – was revealed in 2003, it looked delightful yet impossible (not to mention improbable, given its location in the historically seedy Bowery). New York changes quickly, though, and what once seemed so unlikely (a fine-art museum on a street known for its homeless shelters) now makes sense. It didn't hurt that hip hotel, The Bowery (T 212 505 9100), opened up nearby. After your tour, visit the fun Bowery Diner (T 212 388 0052) next door. *235 Bowery, T 212 219 1222, www.newmuseum.org*

Lincoln Center

To celebrate its 50th anniversary, in 2010, the city's pre-eminent performing arts venue undertook a $1.2bn renovation programme. The aim was to unify the 6.5-hectare complex, creating new spaces and revamping existing buildings, whose original architects included Eero Saarinen, Gordon Bunshaft and Philip Johnson. Diller Scofidio + Renfro and FXFOWLE tackled the overhaul of Alice Tully Hall, part of the 1969 Juilliard School, designed by Pietro Belluschi with Helge Westermann and Eduardo Catalano. The performance facilities have been modernised and a glass-walled foyer has been added to the theatre; the school boasts a transparent, cantilevered canopy, which bursts out of the building towards Broadway. *70 Lincoln Center Plaza, T 212 875 5000, www.lincolncenter.org*

Seagram Building

Mies van der Rohe's 1958 masterpiece typified his less-is-more philosophy and is a triumph of the International Style. In fact, he stated this was his only work in the US that met his stringent European standards of design, borrowed from the architect's classic German Pavilion built for the 1929 Barcelona World's Fair. It was the first building to feature floor-to-ceiling windows to achieve the modernist ideal of a curtain of glass, and although American construction codes prevented him from displaying the structural steel frame, Mies added non-supportive bronze-tinted beams. Despite the austere aesthetic, the extravagant use of materials meant this was the world's most expensive structure at the time. It served as a model for almost every NYC skyscraper that followed.
375 Park Avenue, www.375parkavenue.com

The Morgan Library & Museum

Since JP Morgan Jr donated his father's personal library to the people of New York in 1924, it has to be said that not many of the great unwashed have felt the need to venture in. The collection of Gutenberg Bibles, manuscripts and paintings has always given off enough of an elitist whiff to scare the masses away. Renzo Piano's sublime 2006 expansion added an entrance on Madison Avenue, a glazed atrium and several galleries, increasing the exhibition space by more than 50 per cent – a design intended to beckon people in and pull together the three existing buildings. The Morgan has now become a destination museum and host to swanky, and lucrative, soirées. The old robber baron would have been pleased. *225 Madison Avenue, T 212 685 0008, www.themorgan.org*

FDR Four Freedoms Park

Louis Kahn was commissioned to create a memorial to FDR on Roosevelt Island in 1973. Working with landscape architect Harriet Pattison, Kahn conceived a simple design based on two quintessential forms: the room and the garden. He shaped a 'room' from large granite blocks, creating a serene space on the tip of the island. An extract from FDR's 1941 'Four Freedoms' speech is carved on one wall, behind a 1933 bronze bust of the former president by sculptor Jo Davidson. Two paths lined with linden trees edge the triangular lawn. Kahn's death in 1974 and economic hitches delayed construction until 2010, and the park was opened in October 2012. Poised between Queens and Manhattan, the site is stunning. Open Thursdays to Sundays.
1 FDR Four Freedoms Park, Roosevelt Island, www.fdrfourfreedomspark.org

SHOPPING

THE BEST RETAIL THERAPY AND WHAT TO BUY

Retail therapy is just as crucial as the Jungian variety in helping New Yorkers cope with love, life and the universe. For one-stop shopping, Manhattan's heavy hitters are hard to beat. Barneys (660 Madison Avenue, T 212 826 8900), Saks (611 Fifth Avenue, T 212 753 4000) and Bergdorf Goodman (754 Fifth Avenue, T 212 753 7300) all present an alluring and well-edited mix of established names and up-and-coming labels, whereas Henri Bendel (712 Fifth Avenue, T 212 247 1100) is a destination for beauty junkies.

For a more intimate and original shopping experience, visit independent stores like Cadet (see p084), whose military-inspired menswear is being snapped up by the style-savvy. Fivestory (18 E 69th Street, T 212 288 1338) stocks big-ticket ready-to-wear pieces and accessories for men and women in a handsome townhouse setting. At the other end of the sartorial spectrum, catch the wave of the urban-surf trend (or look as if you know how) at Saturdays Surf (31 Crosby Street, T 212 966 7875) or Pilgrim Surf + Supply (68 N 3rd Street, T 718 218 7456) in Williamsburg.

Design fans should head to Matter (opposite) and The Future Perfect (55 Great Jones Street, T 212 473 2500), which also has a branch in Brooklyn (115 N 6th Street, T 718 599 6278). In Soho, check out Kiosk (see p077) for global curios, and BDDW (5 Crosby Street, T 212 625 1230), which sells handcrafted wooden furniture. *For full addresses, see Resources.*

Matter

Jamie Gray's design emporium debuted in Brooklyn's Park Slope in 2003, opening a Soho branch in 2007, and it excels at presenting a pitch-perfect range of home accessories and furnishings. Gray, a Pratt Institute sculpture graduate, curates the in-house collection, MatterMade, which sits alongside global brands such as French company La Chance, Istanbul collective Autoban and UK designer Faye Toogood.

The proprietor focuses on craftsmanship when he seeks out makers, from glass-blowers to woodworkers. Of those locals currently represented, the work of a clutch of Brooklyn designers caught our eye: Fort Standard's cast-bronze candelabras; Doug Johnston's handmade cord stools; and Fredericks & Mae's quirky objects. *405 Broome Street, T 212 343 2600, www.mattermatters.com*

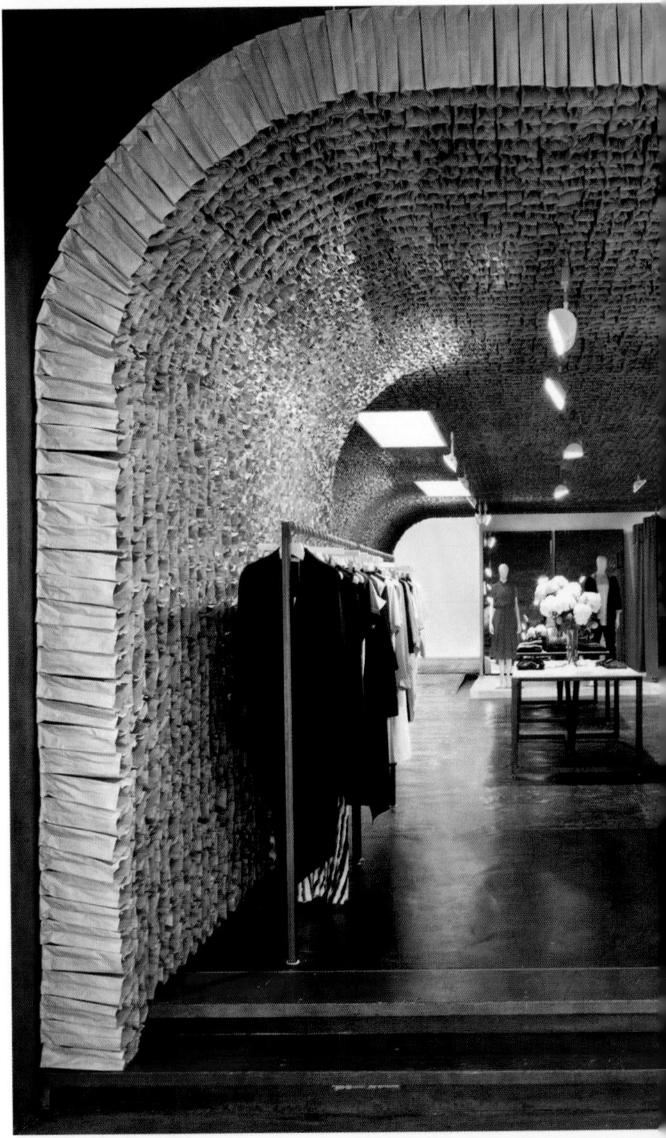

Owen
Young retailer Phillip Salem is holding his own in the saturated Meatpacking District, with his first women's and men's boutique, which opened in 2012 in a former gallery space. Yet it's Jeremy Barbour's interior design – 25,000 brown paper sacks meticulously stapled to the walls – that has grabbed the attention of design and fashion nuts.
809 Washington Street, T 212 524 9770

OHWOW

It may call itself a bookshop, but this tiny store in the West Village is about far more than reading material. Measuring just 18.5 sq m, it's the debut bricks-and-mortar outlet of the bicoastal OHWOW collective. Established in 2008 by Aaron Bondaroff and Al Moran, its aim is to facilitate exhibitions and one-off projects across various media, and publish art-themed books. The eye-popping space,

designed by New York architect Rafael de Cárdenas, was partly inspired by the geometric prints found on traditional Navajo blankets. On the shelves are OHWOW's own books, esteemed style bibles and a selection of accessories. The collective also runs a gallery in Los Angeles (T 310 652 1711).
227 Waverly Place, T 646 370 5847, www.oh-wow.com

Kiosk

Alisa Grifo's brilliant shop/gallery is so delightful because of its selection of everyday objects and its presentation concept: each product comes tagged with its history and provenance. Indeed, Grifo once worked as a curatorial assistant at the Cooper-Hewitt museum, which is currently closed for renovation. There's a mixture of ongoing and one-off items, from a Finnish Abloy padlock to a wood carrier made of vegetable-tanned leather, a collaboration between Kiosk and the US firm Steele Canvas. Bay Rum cologne (above), $22, hails from the Massachusetts-based company Charles H Baldwin & Sons, which has been selling its wares (originally extracts and flavourings) since 1888. Bay Rum is made with oils of bay and clove.
Second floor, 95 Spring Street, T 212 226 8601, www.kioskkiosk.com

Malin+Goetz

Started in New York City in 2004, by
Matthew Malin and Andrew Goetz, the
beauty super-brand Malin+Goetz opened
its second boutique in 2009, in a former
Dominican barbershop on the Upper
West Side. Just like the original branch
in Chelsea (T 212 727 3777), this uptown
store has the feel of a contemporary
apothecary and boasts a unique interior.
Brooklyn architect Craig Konyk installed
rich, walnut panels, salvaged from a Long
Island mansion, which he juxtaposed
with clinical white counters. Some of
the shop's original features, such as the
tin ceiling, were maintained. The products
smell gorgeous and are aimed at those
with sensitive skin. M+G launched a Los
Angeles outpost (T 323 391 1884) in 2012.
*455 Amsterdam Avenue, T 212 799 1200,
www.malinandgoetz.com*

Billy Reid

Alabama-based William Reid had his first New York moment about a decade ago, when his suits and casualwear won a quiet following among NYC's sharpest dressers. He opened this store in 2008, selling his fine-woven blazers, chinos, corduroy jackets and Oxford shirts, plus a capsule collection of womenswear. Although it's in the heart of Gotham, the boutique displays Reid's Southern touch; there are vintage cabinets, a couch constructed from church pews, and a ceiling panelled with doors that were salvaged from a Mississippi schoolhouse. It's a civilised shop for the civilised shopper. A plaudit as Menswear Designer of the Year at the 2012 CFDA Awards bolstered the appeal of Billy Reid's clothing for dapper New York gents. *54 Bond Street, T 212 598 9355, www.billyreid.com*

Creatures of Comfort

Nolita has never lacked a good sprinkling of interesting retail outlets, but the launch of Creatures of Comfort in 2010 brought a new sense of vitality to this popular area. An eclectic mix of products is presented in the sprawling 230 sq m exposed-brick store, overseen by buyer and owner Jade Lai, who started the company in Los Angeles. Lai lures shoppers with goods spanning Japanese furniture to Bernhard Willhelm nail varnish. Best of all, though, is the fashion, mostly the womenswear, with the company's own ready-to-wear sitting alongside clothes by Slow and Steady Wins the Race, Isabel Marant and Henrik Vibskov, among others. There's also a project space in the shop, which hosts pop-ups, exhibitions and events. *205 Mulberry Street, T 212 925 1005, www.creaturesofcomfort.us*

Hollander & Lexer
H&L's second Brooklyn boutique sells
trend-resistant and vintage items: a
sartorial mix that sealed the success
of the first shop in Park Slope. Peruse
the own-brand menswear and range of
accessories, such as Japanese scrubbing
brushes. Owners Yaz Benmira and Brian
Cousins designed the interior, which
has a fabulous antique appearance.
103 Metropolitan Avenue, T 718 797 9117

Cadet

This crisp Brooklyn boutique, which has an interior punctuated with ammunition belts, vintage globes and a portrait of a Civil War general, reinforces the military-inspired look for which menswear label Cadet has gained street cred. Although owners Raul Arevalo and Brad Schmidt appreciate the precise lines and timeless appeal of historic uniforms, they apply a modern spin to their clothes. Wardrobe basics such as button-down shirts and trousers are most popular, and customers take full advantage of the free alteration service. Everything is designed and made at Cadet's factory in Bushwick, and sold only in its own stores. If you can't make it to Williamsburg, visit the newer East Village shop (T 646 633 4560).
46 N 6th Street, T 718 715 1695,
www.cadetusa.com

Alexander Wang

A luxe but relaxed aesthetic has rendered Alexander Wang's womenswear a fashion-pack staple. Opened in 2011, on Soho's grungy-glam Grand Street, his Ryan Korban-designed flagship store is a mix of boutique, gallery and design den. The large, all-white space has high ceilings, marble floors and an oversized steel cage covered by seasonal installations. After browsing through Wang's sexy, downtown-friendly clothing and accessories, head to the centre of the shop, where a lounging area beckons you to kick off your heels or, considering the environs, your Converse. The leather sofa and brass table laden with books and magazines will ease any retail fatigue, as will the fox-fur hammock: simple but sumptuous, à la Wang. *103 Grand Street, T 212 977 9683, www.alexanderwang.com*

RePOP

It didn't take very long for vintage-design purveyor RePOP to outgrow its original store in Brooklyn's Clinton Hill. To meet the surge in demand for his wares, which he sources from across the US, owner Russell Boyle moved to a larger location in Williamsburg in 2012, a 148 sq m space in the same building as Roebling Tea Room (see p040). The airy showroom is packed with items from various eras, and makes for inspiring browsing as a result. It's worth spending at least an hour or so here so you can scour the stock properly. Covetable finds on our visit ranged from antique dress dummies to original Danish Modern dressers and one-off lighting fixtures. RePOP's prices are fairer than you'll find in Manhattan, and bargaining isn't ruled out. Boyle also offers personal design consultations by appointment.
143 Roebling Street, T 718 260 8032, www.repopny.com

SPORTS AND SPAS

WORK OUT, CHILL OUT OR JUST WATCH

From manicurists to masseurs, pedicurists to personal trainers, the Manhattanite has a small army of auxiliary support at his or her disposal, making this the ideal city for the beauty tourist. Among the quick-service salons popping up around town, Gotham Beauty Lounge (32 W 40th Street, T 212 921 2002) in Midtown is perfect for a speedy facial and an expert make-up application; guys can get a haircut and a hot shave at Decatur & Sons Barber Shop (75 Ninth Avenue, T 646 470 7288). Nobody pampers hands and feet better than Jin Soon Hand & Foot Spa (156 E 4th Street, T 212 473 2047), while The Spa at Mandarin Oriental (80 Columbus Circle, T 212 805 8880) provides holistic treatments in a sky-high setting.

For a serious workout, spinning is still popular – try the Tribeca branch of SoulCycle (103 Warren Street, T 212 406 1300) or the trendy new Aqua (see p090). Continue the good work at home with skincare from classic American brands Kiehl's (157 E 64th Street, T 917 432 2503) or Malin+Goetz (see p078), and conceptual scents from CB I Hate Perfume (93 Wythe Avenue, T 718 384 6890).

The city has a plethora of gyms, most of which issue day passes. Otherwise, Central Park is the place to pound the pounds, or along the Hudson. Catch the Knicks shooting hoops at Madison Square Garden (4 Pennsylvania Plaza, T 212 465 6741), and baseball at the Yankee Stadium in the Bronx (1 E 161st Street, T 718 293 6000). *For full addresses, see Resources.*

Cornelia Spa at The Surrey

There are plenty of luxurious spas in New York, but none that feel quite as discreet as this one. On the second floor of The Surrey hotel, Cornelia was designed by Lauren Rottet, who has done a fine job of carving out a chic relaxation area (above) and five well-appointed rooms within a tight space. Before your session, there are some thoughtful touches – a warm ginger-scented hand towel, a herbal neck pillow, a spoonful of artisanal honey, and a bar of delicate snacks, which are prepared by the spa's own chef. Before you leave, you will be offered nibbles to complement your treatment. To ensure the utmost privacy, there is no common changing area. Instead, each room comes equipped with a private armoire.
20 E 76th Street, T 646 358 3600,
www.corneliaspaatthesurrey.com

Aqua

French expat Esther Gauthier brought her native country's latest fitness craze stateside to Tribeca. Aqua spinning, which involves underwater cycling, provides a low-impact, high-resistance workout, which, according to its devotees, reduces stress on joints and tones up cellulite. David Obuchowski, of DO Architecture, joined forces with Gauthier to create a studio that feels minimal and spa-like, thanks to the blend of concrete, brick and wood. The entrance area is a real success, with its oak flooring and contemporary lighting; the darkwood changing rooms have a monochromatic scheme. The pool room is sparse yet bright, with white brick walls and a lofty ceiling. Launched in 2013, Aqua is currently open to women only. *78 Franklin Street, T 212 966 6784, www.aquastudiony.com*

Takamichi Hair

Stepping into Takamichi Saeki's second-floor studio on the Bowery, it can be tricky to fathom what he's all about, which in this case is no bad thing. The gallerist-turned-hair-stylist enlisted friends and colleagues to convert the 186 sq m space into this striking salon, which could double as an art space. Belgian architect Sandra van Rolleghem pays tribute to 1960s Scandinavian style with streamlined white chairs and punchy red accents. Art by Santi Moix and Richard Hambleton graces the walls, and Belgian designer Éric Guen's origami chandeliers hang at the entrance. The owner's signature 'Takamichi Cut' is tailored to your head shape, texture and lifestyle. You'll leave feeling like the venue – one of a kind. Closed Mondays.
Second floor, 263 Bowery, T 212 420 7979, www.takamichihair.com

The Spa at Trump Soho

Looking down on Spring Street from Trump Soho's seventh floor, this spa combines old-world cleansing rituals with modern luxury. Ivanka Trump hired architects DiGuiseppe to construct the spa, and the standard is set by an entrance adorned with a fountain carved from Calacatta gold marble, a crystal and nickel woven-mesh chandelier, and a Macassar ebony doorway. But it's the hammam, the very first in New York, that takes top billing. Hand-tiled with Turkish and Moroccan materials, its domed ceiling has pinholes, echoing the classic traditional design. For the *gommage*, attendants use *kese* mitts for exfoliation, and *torba* (cotton soap pouches) to work up a lather. Afterwards, soothing mint tea awaits on a lush terrace. *246 Spring Street, T 212 842 5500, www.trumphotelcollection.com*

Rudy's Barbershop

For their first East Coast branch, on the ground floor of the Ace Hotel (see p020), the owners of Rudy's (Wade Weigel, Alex Calderwood and David Petersen) wanted a salon with unisex appeal. Aiming for a utilitarian but quirky feel, they began the process with Brooklyn-based WRK Design, sourcing fixtures from a former Remington Arms factory in Connecticut. They also scoured New York for items such as the baked enamel wall panels and vintage lighting, both found on the Bowery. A long outdoor bench and tiny private garden were added, so you can socialise before and after your haircut. Post-appointment, visit the retail space upstairs, stocked with grooming products by Baxter, accessories by Poler, and a reading selection curated by art bookstore Karma (T 917 675 7508). *14 W 29th Street, T 212 532 7200, www.rudysbarbershop.com*

ESCAPES

WHERE TO GO IF YOU WANT TO LEAVE TOWN

Gothamites claim that when you leave New York, you ain't going nowhere – although in summer, the city's border seems to stretch to include the length of Long Island. When the going gets hot, the hot crowd gets going. (If you can stand the humidity in town, your reward will be blissfully empty shops and restaurants.) Escape options are plentiful, whether your taste is for an art expedition (opposite and p102), surfing off Montauk – stay at The Surf Lodge (183 Edgemere Street, T 631 668 1562) or Ruschmeyer's (161 Second House Road, T 631 668 2877) – or hiking in the Catskills. Upstate, the charming eight-room inn, Bedford Post (954 Old Post Road, Bedford, T 914 234 7800), is only an hour's drive from Manhattan.

If you visit the Hamptons, make sure you have a friend with a house, or book well in advance. Get there on the Hampton Jitney (www.hamptonjitney.com), whose glamorous passengers give new meaning to coach travel, or endure the bumper-to-bumper drive. In Bridgehampton, Topping Rose House (One Bridgehampton, Sag Harbor Turnpike, T 631 537 0870), with its restaurant headed by Tom Colicchio, is a smart place to stay. Shelter Island is less intense; go by ferry and stay at André Balazs' Sunset Beach hotel (35 Shore Road, T 631 749 2001). Closer to home, Brighton Beach and Coney Island, known as Little Odessa, are more Moscow than Manhattan, so pack a Russian phrase book with your towel.
For full addresses, see Resources.

Dia:Beacon, Riggio Galleries

The Dia Art Foundation has supported artists since 1974. Its art collection is housed in an old Nabisco box factory in Beacon, remodelled by New York firm OpenOffice and artist Robert Irwin. The collection includes pieces by Walter De Maria, Michael Heizer and Richard Serra (*Torqued Ellipse II* and *Double Torqued Ellipse*, above). Rather than creating a Guggenheim-esque shell that risked overshadowing the art, the architects designed a loft-like space; in fact, this is where many artworks are created. Make it a day trip (it's an 80-minute train ride from Grand Central Station) and combine with a visit to the Richard B Fisher Center (T 845 758 7914), which is further up the valley. Closed Tuesdays and Wednesdays. *3 Beekman Street, Beacon, T 845 440 0100, www.diabeacon.org*

Noguchi Museum
Isamu Noguchi set up a studio and home
in Queens in 1960, which now form part
of this museum. Here you can view a
broad range of the artist's work, such as
his set designs for the dancer Martha
Graham. The tranquil garden, with some
of his sculptures, weeping cherry trees
and bamboo, is worth the trip alone.
9-01 33rd Road, Long Island City,
T 718 204 7088, www.noguchi.org

Glass House, New Canaan
The Connecticut town of New Canaan, about 40 miles north-east of NYC, boasts some of the finest examples of modern American architecture. The most famous is Philip Johnson's home, the Glass House (pictured), which he completed in 1949. It is perhaps the purest example of the International Style. Call in advance.
Visitor Center, 199 Elm Street, T 866 811 4111, www.philipjohnsonglasshouse.org

Parrish Art Museum, Long Island

Artists have populated Long Island's East End since the late 19th century, when commuting from New York was made easier by an extension of the Long Island Rail Road. Notable figures have been drawn by the light and the beauty of the landscape, from Impressionist William Merritt Chase to abstract expressionists Jackson Pollock and Willem de Kooning. The Parrish Art Museum was founded in Southampton in 1898, by collector Samuel Longstreth Parrish. In 2012, it relocated to a new building by Herzog & de Meuron. Modelled on an East End artist's studio, and featuring two striking overhangs, the sky-lit space has tripled the exhibition area for the permanent collection of early 19th-century to present-day East End art. *279 Montauk Highway, Water Mill, T 631 283 2118, www.parrishart.org*

NOTES

SKETCHES AND MEMOS

RESOURCES

CITY GUIDE DIRECTORY

A

Alder 046
157 Second Avenue
T 212 539 1900
www.aldernyc.com

Alexander Wang 085
103 Grand Street
T 212 977 9683
www.alexanderwang.com

The Americano 017
Hôtel Americano
518 W 27th Street
T 212 525 0000
www.hotel-americano.com

Antica Pesa 041
115 Berry Street
Brooklyn
T 347 763 2635
www.anticapesa.com

Aqua 090
78 Franklin Street
T 212 966 6784
www.aquastudiony.com

Arlington Club 038
1032 Lexington Avenue
T 212 249 5700
www.arlingtonclubny.com

Aska 040
90 Wythe Avenue
Brooklyn
T 718 388 2969
www.askanyc.com

AT&T Building 012
32 Sixth Avenue
www.32sixthave.com

Atera 052
77 Worth Street
T 212 226 1444
www.ateranyc.com

Austrian Cultural Forum 014
11 E 52nd Street
T 212 319 5300
www.acfny.org

B

Babbo 050
110 Waverley Place
T 212 777 0303
www.babbonyc.com

Barneys 072
660 Madison Avenue
T 212 826 8900
www.barneys.com

BDDW 072
5 Crosby Street
T 212 625 1230
www.bddw.com

Bergdorf Goodman 072
754 Fifth Avenue
T 212 753 7300
www.bergdorfgoodman.com

Billy Reid 080
54 Bond Street
T 212 598 9355
www.billyreid.com

Blue Ribbon 062
97 Sullivan Street
T 212 274 0404
www.blueribbonrestaurants.com

Blue Ribbon Sushi Izakaya 016
Thompson LES
190 Allen Street
T 212 466 0404
www.thompsonhotels.com

Bobo 050
181 W 10th Street
T 212 488 2626
www.bobonyc.com

Bouchon Bakery 033
Third floor
Time Warner Center
10 Columbus Circle
T 212 823 9366
www.bouchonbakery.com
The Bowery Diner 065
241 Bowery
T 212 388 0052
www.bowerydiner.com
Bread 062
20 Spring Street
T 212 334 1015
Brushstroke 053
30 Hudson Street
T 212 791 3771
www.davidbouley.com

C
Cadet 084
46 N 6th Street
Brooklyn
T 718 715 1695
305 E 9th Street
T 646 633 4560
www.cadetusa.com
Café Boulud 016
The Surrey
20 E 76th Street
T 212 772 2600
www.cafeboulud.com
Carbone 040
181 Thompson Street
T 212 254 3000
www.carbonenewyork.com
CB I Hate Perfume 088
93 Wythe Avenue
Brooklyn
T 718 384 6890
www.cbihateperfume.com

Center Bar 040
Fourth floor
Time Warner Center
10 Columbus Circle
T 212 823 9482
www.centerbarnyc.com
Chrysler Building 064
405 Lexington Avenue
Cornelia Spa at The Surrey 089
The Surrey
20 E 76th Street
T 646 358 3600
www.corneliaspaatthesurrey.com
Creatures of Comfort 081
205 Mulberry Street
T 212 925 1005
www.creaturesofcomfort.us

D
David Burke Kitchen 029
The James
23 Grand Street
T 212 201 9119
www.davidburkekitchen.com
Decatur & Sons Barber Shop 088
Chelsea Market
75 Ninth Avenue
T 646 470 7288
www.decaturandsons.com
Dia:Beacon, Riggio Galleries 097
3 Beekman Street
Beacon
T 845 440 0100
www.diabeacon.org
Donna 060
27 Broadway
Brooklyn
T 646 568 6622
www.donnabklyn.com

E

Edi & The Wolf 057
102 Avenue C
T 212 598 1040
www.ediandthewolf.com
Eleven Madison Park 025
11 Madison Avenue
T 212 889 0905
www.elevenmadisonpark.com
Espasso 054
38 N Moore Street
T 212 219 0017
www.espasso.com

F

4 WTC 009
150 Greenwich Street
www.wtc.com
FDR Four Freedoms Park 070
1 FDR Four Freedoms Park
Roosevelt Island
www.fdrfourfreedomspark.org
Fivestory 072
18 E 69th Street
T 212 288 1338
www.fivestoryny.com
The Future Perfect 072
55 Great Jones Street
T 212 473 2500
115 N 6th Street
Brooklyn
T 718 599 6278
www.thefutureperfect.com

G

Gavin Brown's Enterprise 062
620 Greenwich Street
T 212 627 5258
www.gavinbrown.biz

Ginny's Supper Club 059
310 Lenox Avenue
T 212 421 3821
www.ginnyssupperclub.com
Glass House 100
Visitor Center
199 Elm Street
New Canaan
Connecticut
T 866 811 4111
www.philipjohnsonglasshouse.org
Gotham Beauty Lounge 088
32 W 40th Street
T 212 921 2002
www.gothambeautylounge.com
Guggenheim 032
1071 Fifth Avenue
T 212 423 3500
www.guggenheim.org

H

Hearst Tower 013
300 W 57th Street
www.hearst.com
Henri Bendel 072
712 Fifth Avenue
T 212 247 1100
www.henribendel.com
High Line 036
T 212 500 6035
www.thehighline.org
Hollander & Lexer 082
103 Metropolitan Avenue
Brooklyn
T 718 797 9117
www.hollanderandlexer.com
Hospoda 049
321 E 73rd Street
T 212 861 1038
www.hospodanyc.com

I
Irving Trust Company HQ 012
1 Wall Street

J
Jin Soon Hand & Foot Spa 088
156 E 4th Street
T 212 473 2047
www.jinsoon.com

K
Karma 095
39 Great Jones Street
T 917 675 7508
www.karmakarma.org
Kiehl's 088
157 E 64th Street
T 917 432 2503
www.kiehls.com
Kiosk 077
Second floor
95 Spring Street
T 212 226 8601
www.kisokkiosk.com

L
The Lambs Club 031
The Chatwal
132 W 44th Street
T 212 997 5262
www.thelambsclub.com
Lehmann Maupin 062
540 W 26th Street
T 212 255 2923
www.lehmannmaupin.com
Lincoln Center 066
70 Lincoln Center Plaza
T 212 875 5000
www.lincolncenter.org

Luksus 040
615 Manhattan Avenue
Brooklyn
T 718 389 6034
www.torstnyc.com

M
Má Pêche 048
15 W 56th Street
T 212 757 5878
www.momofuku.com
Madison Square Garden 088
4 Pennsylvania Plaza
T 212 465 6741
www.thegarden.com
Maison Kitsuné 025
The NoMad Hotel
1170 Broadway
T 212 481 6010
www.kitsune.fr
Malin+Goetz 078
455 Amsterdam Avenue
T 212 799 1200
177 Seventh Avenue
T 212 727 3777
238 N Larchmont Boulevard
Los Angeles
T 323 391 1884
www.malinandgoetz.com
Matter 073
405 Broome Street
T 212 343 2600
www.mattermatters.com
Metropolitan Museum of Art 032
1000 Fifth Avenue
T 212 535 7710
www.metmuseum.org

Milano's Bar 062
51 E Houston Street
T 212 226 8844
Miss Lily's 056
132 W Houston Street
T 646 588 5375
www.misslilysnyc.com
MoMA 032
11 W 53rd Street
T 212 708 9400
www.moma.org
MoMA PS1 034
22-25 Jackson Avenue
Queens
T 718 784 2084
www.momaps1.org
Momofuku Ssäm Bar 048
207 Second Avenue
T 212 254 3500
www.momofuku.com
The Morgan Library & Museum 069
225 Madison Avenue
T 212 685 0008
www.themorgan.org

N
9/11 Memorial 010
Albany Street/Greenwich Street
T 212 266 5211
www.911memorial.org
National September 11
Memorial Museum 009
Albany Street/Greenwich Street
T 212 266 5211
www.911memorial.org/museum
New Museum 065
235 Bowery
T 212 219 1222
www.newmuseum.org

New York Public Library 064
42nd Street/Fifth Avenue
T 917 275 6975
www.nypl.org
Noguchi Museum 098
9-01 33rd Road
Queens
T 718 204 7088
www.noguchi.org
NoMad 025
The NoMad Hotel
1170 Broadway
T 347 472 5660
www.thenomadhotel.com

O
1 WTC 009
West Street/Vesey Street
www.onewtc.com
OHWOW 076
227 Waverly Place
T 646 370 5847
937 N La Cienega Boulevard
Los Angeles
T 310 652 1711
www.oh-wow.com
Owen 074
809 Washington Street
T 212 524 9770
www.owennyc.com

P
El Parador Café 062
325 E 34th Street
T 212 679 6812
www.elparadorcafe.com

Parrish Art Museum 102
279 Montauk Highway
Water Mill
Long Island
T 631 283 2118
www.parrishart.org
Pearl & Ash 042
220 Bowery
T 212 837 2370
www.pearlandash.com
Per Se 033
Fourth floor
Time Warner Center
10 Columbus Circle
T 212 823 9335
www.perseny.com
Pilgrim Surf + Supply 072
68 N 3rd Street
Brooklyn
T 718 218 7456
www.pilgrimsurfsupply.com
La Piscine 054
Hôtel Americano
518 W 27th Street
T 212 525 0000
www.hotel-americano.com
Potlikker 045
338 Bedford Avenue
Brooklyn
T 718 388 9808
www.potlikkerbrooklyn.com
Proenza Schouler 037
822 Madison Avenue
T 212 585 3200
www.proenzaschouler.com

R
Red Rooster 058
310 Lenox Avenue
T 212 792 9001
www.redroosterharlem.com
RePOP 086
143 Roebling Street
Brooklyn
T 718 260 8032
www.repopny.com
Reynard 027
Wythe Hotel
80 Wythe Avenue
Brooklyn
T 718 460 8004
www.wythehotel.com
**Richard B Fisher Center for the
Performing Arts at Bard College** 097
Annandale-on-Hudson
T 845 758 7914
www.fishercenter.bard.edu
River Styx 040
21 Greenpoint Avenue
Brooklyn
Roebling Tea Room 040
143 Roebling Street
Brooklyn
T 718 963 0760
www.roeblingtearoom.com
Rosemary's 050
18 Greenwich Avenue
T 212 647 1818
www.rosemarysnyc.com
Rudy's Barbershop 094
14 W 29th Street
T 212 532 7200
www.rudysbarbershop.com

Runner & Stone 033
285 3rd Avenue
Brooklyn
T 718 576 3360
www.runnerandstone.com

S
S Prime 040
35-15 36th Street
Queens
T 718 707 0660
www.sprimenyc.com
Saks 072
611 Fifth Avenue
T 212 753 4000
www.saksfifthavenue.com
Salon 94 Bowery 062
243 Bowery
T 212 979 0001
www.salon94.com
Saturdays Surf 072
31 Crosby Street
T 212 966 7875
www.saturdaysnyc.com
Seagram Building 068
375 Park Avenue
www.375parkavenue.com
Seäsonal 057
132 W 58th Street
T 212 957 5550
www.seasonalnyc.com
Souen 062
326 E 6th Street
T 212 388 1155
www.souen.net
SoulCycle 088
103 Warren Street
T 212 406 1300
www.soul-cycle.com

The Spa at Mandarin Oriental 088
Mandarin Oriental
80 Columbus Circle
T 212 805 8880
www.mandarinoriental.com/newyork
The Spa at Trump Soho 093
Trump Soho
246 Spring Street
T 212 842 5500
www.trumphotelcollection.com
The Standard Grill 030
The Standard High Line
848 Washington Street
T 212 645 4100
www.thestandardgrill.com

T
Takamichi Hair 092
Second floor
263 Bowery
T 212 420 7979
www.takamichihair.com
Talde 044
369 7th Avenue
Brooklyn
T 347 916 0031
www.taldebrooklyn.com
The Third Man 057
116 Avenue C
T 212 598 1040
www.thethirdmannyc.com
Tribeca Canvas 040
313 Church Street
T 917 720 2845
www.tribecacanvasnyc.com

W
Wall & Water 022
 Andaz Wall Street
 75 Wall Street
 T 212 699 1700
 www.andaz.com
Whitney Museum of American Art 032
 945 Madison Avenue
 T 212 570 3600
 www.whitney.org
Woolworth Building 015
 233 Broadway

Y
Yankee Stadium 088
 1 E 161st Street
 T 718 293 6000
 www.yankees.com

HOTELS

ADDRESSES AND ROOM RATES

Ace Hotel 020
Room rates:
double, $415;
Loft 811, $2,300
20 W 29th Street
T 212 679 2222
www.acehotel.com

Hôtel Americano 017
Room rates:
double, from $305;
Studio Suite, from $575
518 W 27th Street
T 212 216 0000
www.hotel-americano.com

Andaz Wall Street 022
Room rates:
double, from $395;
Room 1513, from $395
75 Wall Street
T 212 590 1234
www.andaz.com

Bedford Post 096
Room rates:
double, from $545
954 Old Post Road
Bedford
T 914 234 7800
www.bedfordpostinn.com

The Bowery Hotel 065
Room rates:
double, from $335
335 Bowery
T 212 505 9100
www.theboweryhotel.com

The Chatwal 031
Room rates:
double, from $795;
Producer Suite, from $3,795
130 W 44th Street
T 212 764 6200
www.thechatwalny.com

Crosby Street Hotel 024
Room rates:
double, from $555;
One Bedroom Suite, from $1,950
79 Crosby Street
T 212 226 6400
www.firmdalehotels.com

Four Seasons 023
Room rates:
double, from $800;
Ty Warner Penthouse, $45,900
57 E 57th Street
T 212 758 5700
www.fourseasons.com/newyork

The Jade Hotel 018
Room rates:
double, from $400;
Standard Room, from $400
52 W 13th Street
T 212 375 1300
www.thejadenyc.com

The James 029
Room rates:
double, from $415
27 Grand Street
T 212 465 2000
www.jameshotel.com

The Mercer 030
Room rates:
double, from $595
147 Mercer Street
T 212 966 6060
www.mercerhotel.com

The Nolitan 028
Room rates:
double, from $380
30 Kenmare Street
T 212 925 2555
www.nolitanhotel.com

The NoMad Hotel 025
Room rates:
double, from $390;
Grande Room, $650;
Suite, from $685
1170 Broadway
T 212 796 1500
www.thenomadhotel.com

The Quin 016
Room rates:
double, from $495
101 W 57th Street
T 212 600 2108
www.thequinhotel.com

Refinery Hotel 016
Room rates:
double, from $450
63 W 38th Street
T 646 664 0310
www.refineryhotelnewyork.com

Ruschmeyer's 096
Room rates:
double, $195
161 Second House Road
Montauk
Long Island
T 631 668 2877
www.kingandgrove.com

The Standard High Line 030
Room rates:
double, from $340
848 Washington Street
T 212 645 4646
www.standardhotels.com/high-line

Sunset Beach 096
Room rates:
double, from $345
35 Shore Road
Shelter Island
T 631 749 2001
www.sunsetbeachli.com

The Surf Lodge 096
Room rates:
double, from $515
183 Edgemere Street
Montauk
Long Island
T 631 668 1562
www.thesurflodge.com

The Surrey 016
Room rates:
double, from $570
20 E 76th Street
T 212 288 3700
www.thesurrey.com

Thompson LES 016
Room rates:
double, from $280
190 Allen Street
T 212 460 5300
www.thompsonhotels.com

Topping Rose House 096
Room rates:
double, from $1,050
One Bridgehampton
Sag Harbor Turnpike
Long Island
T 631 537 0870
www.toppingrosehouse.com

Wythe Hotel 026
Room rates:
double, from $260;
Manhattan View King Room, from $405
80 Wythe Avenue
Brooklyn
T 718 460 8000
www.wythehotel.com

WALLPAPER* CITY GUIDES

Executive Editor
Rachael Moloney

Author
Katie Chang

Art Director
Loran Stosskopf
Art Editor
Eriko Shimazaki
Designer
Mayumi Hashimoto
Map Illustrator
Russell Bell

Photography Editor
Elisa Merlo
Assistant Photography Editor
Nabil Butt

Chief Sub-Editor
Nick Mee
Sub-Editor
Farah Shafiq

Editorial Assistant
Emma Harrison

Intern
Sara Bellini

Wallpaper* Group Editor-in-Chief
Tony Chambers
Publishing Director
Gord Ray
Managing Editor
Oliver Adamson

Contributor
David Kaufman

Wallpaper* ® is a registered trademark of IPC Media Limited

First published 2006
Revised and updated 2008, 2009, 2010, 2011 and 2013

All prices are correct at the time of going to press, but are subject to change.

Printed in China

PHAIDON

Phaidon Press Limited
Regent's Wharf
All Saints Street
London N1 9PA

Phaidon Press Inc
180 Varick Street
New York, NY 10014

Phaidon® is a registered trademark of Phaidon Press Limited

www.phaidon.com

© 2006, 2008, 2009, 2010, 2011 and 2013
IPC Media Limited

ISBN 978 0 7148 6628 4

PHOTOGRAPHERS

Iwan Baan
High Line, p036

Richard Barnes
Dia:Beacon, Riggio
Galleries, p097

Magda Biernat
Hôtel Americano, p017
Talde, p044
La Piscine, pp054-055
Red Rooster, p058, p059
Donna, pp060-061
Lincoln Center, pp066-067
Matter, p073
Hollander & Lexer,
pp082-083
Takamichi Hair, p092
The Spa at Trump
Soho, p093
Rudy's Barbershop,
pp094-095

Ron Blunt
Glass House, pp100-101

Roger Casas
New York city view,
inside front cover
Hearst Tower, p013
Austrian Cultural
Forum, p014
Woolworth Building, p015
Seagram Building, p068
Billy Reid, p080

Elizabeth Felicella
Noguchi Museum,
pp098-099

Baldomero Fernandez
The Chatwal, p031
Creatures of Comfort, p081

Floto+Warner Studio
The Nolitan, p028
OHWOW, p076

Hotelexistence.com
Andaz Wall Street, p022

Noah Kalina
Momofuko Ssäm Bar, p048

Dean Kaufman
New Museum, p065

Nikolas Koenig
Ace Hotel, pp020-021

Eric Laignel
Malin+Goetz, pp078-079

Christoph Morlinghaus
The Standard High
Line, p030

**Courtesy of The
NoMad Hotel**
The NoMad Hotel, p025

Fran Parente
9/11 Memorial, pp010-011
The Jade Hotel, p018, p019
Runner & Stone, p033
MoMA PS1, p034, p035
Proenza Schouler, p037
Arlington Club, pp038-039
Antica Pesa, p041
Pearl & Ash, pp042-043
Potlikker, p045
Alder, pp046-047
Hospoda, p049
Rosemary's, pp050-051
Atera, p052
The Third Man, p057
Andrea Mary
Marshall, p063
Cadet, p084
RePOP, pp086-087
Cornelia Spa at
The Surrey, p089
Aqua, pp090-091

Matthu Placek
Parrish Art
Museum, pp102-103

Annie Schlechter
Four Seasons, p023

Paul Warchol
FDR Four Freedoms
Park, pp070-071

Courtesy of Wythe Hotel
Wythe Hotel, pp026-027

NEW YORK

A COLOUR-CODED GUIDE TO THE HOT 'HOODS

TRIBECA/THE BATTERY
Lower Manhattan embraces Wall Street and, to the north, hip stores and restaurants

UPPER WEST SIDE
This is Woody Allen territory, characterised by the apartment blocks of the bourgeoisie

WEST VILLAGE
This charming district has tree-lined streets, and plenty of chichi boutiques and eateries

SOHO
Fashion flagships draw the tourists, but there are interesting galleries and shops here too

UPPER EAST SIDE
Visit the swanky shops of Madison Avenue and some of the best museums in the world

MIDTOWN
The throbbing business heart of New York is the location of the neon-tastic Times Square

CHELSEA
New York's power art crowd gather day and night in this slick West Side neighbourhood

EAST VILLAGE/LOWER EAST SIDE
Super-cool bars, stores and galleries pepper this increasingly affluent part of town

For a full description of each neighbourhood, see the Introduction.
Featured venues are colour-coded, according to the district in which they are located.